HAL•LEONARD® KEYBOARD PLAY-ALONG

1950s Rock

ISBN 978-1-4234-6183-8

HAL•LEONARD®
CORPORATION
7777 W. BLUEMOUND RD. P.O. BOX 13819 MILWAUKEE, WI 53213

Visit Hal Leonard Online at
www.halleonard.com

Blueberry Hill

Words and Music by Al Lewis, Larry Stock and Vincent Rose

The moon stood still __ on _____ Blue-ber - ry Hill, ___ and lin - gered un - til __ my dream __ came __ true. The wind in ___ the

Good Golly Miss Molly

Words and Music by Robert Blackwell and John Marascalco

Fast Rock Shuffle

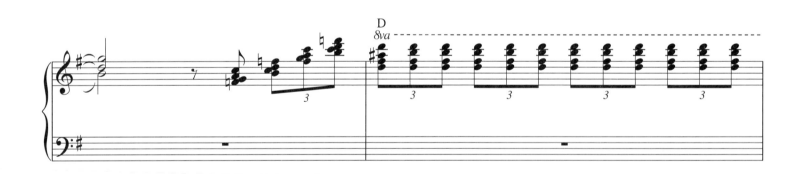

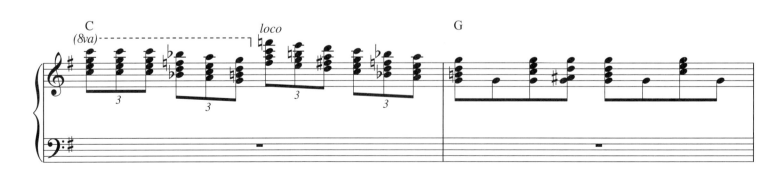

I can't hear your ma - ma call.

Ah!

Sax solo ad lib.

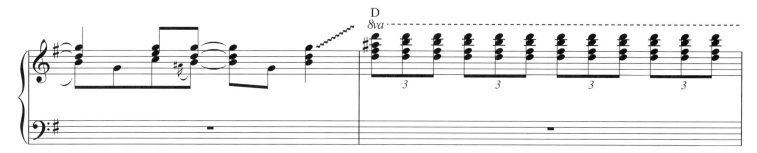

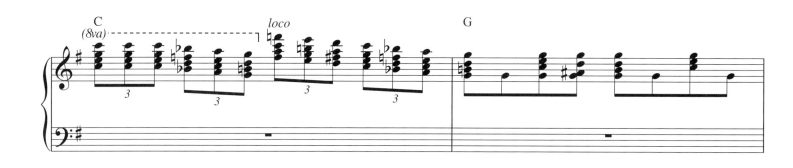

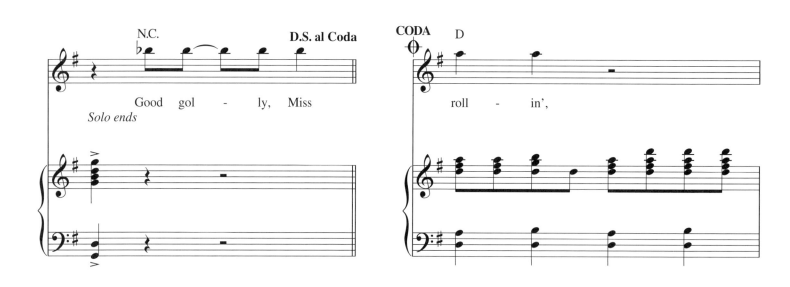

Good gol - ly, Miss

Solo ends

roll - in',

I can't hear your ma - ma call.

Great Balls of Fire

Words and Music by Otis Blackwell and Jack Hammer

Fast Rock 'n' Roll

You shake my nerves and you rat-tle my brain.

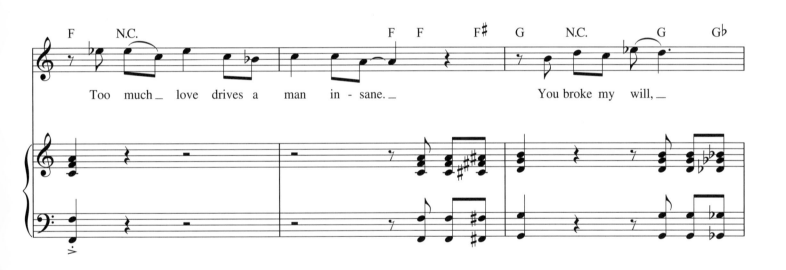

Too much love drives a man in-sane. You broke my will,

but what a thrill. Good-ness, gra-cious, great balls of fi-re!

To Coda ⊕

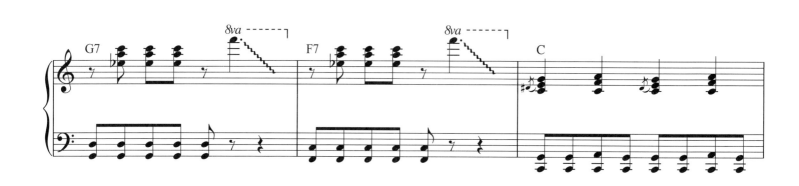

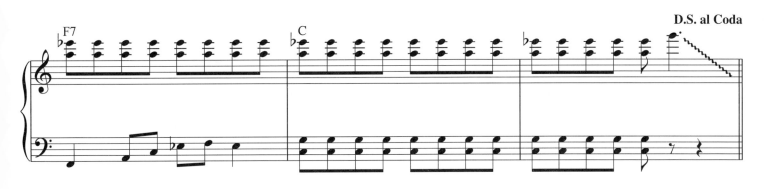

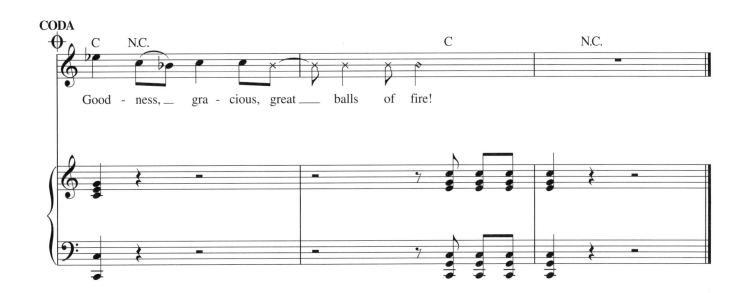

Good - ness, __ gra - cious, great ___ balls of fire!

The Great Pretender
Words and Music by Buck Ram

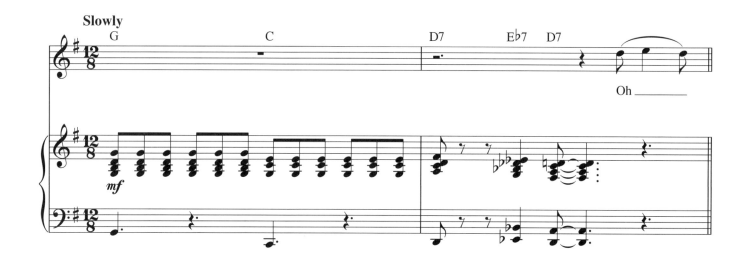

Rock and Roll Is Here to Stay

Words and Music by David White

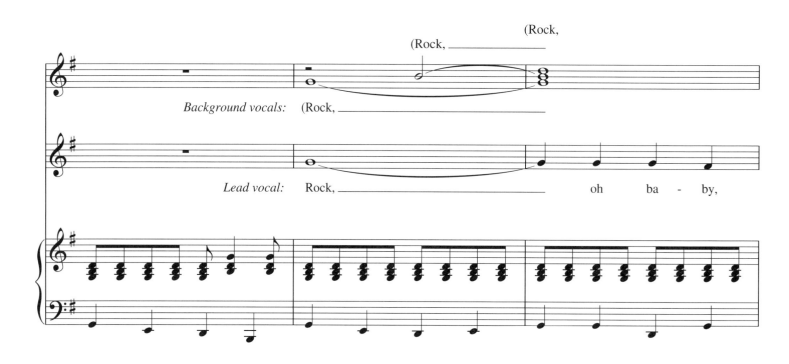

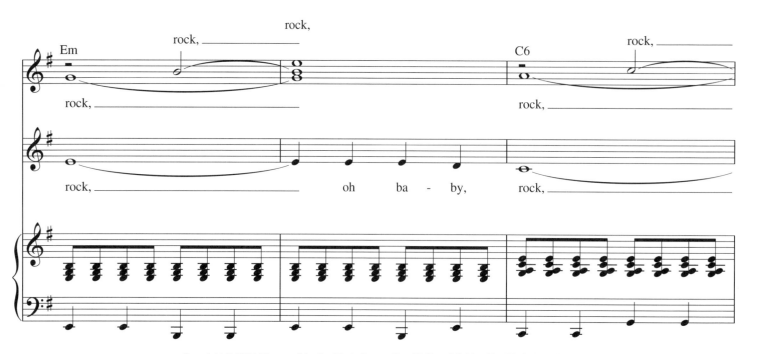

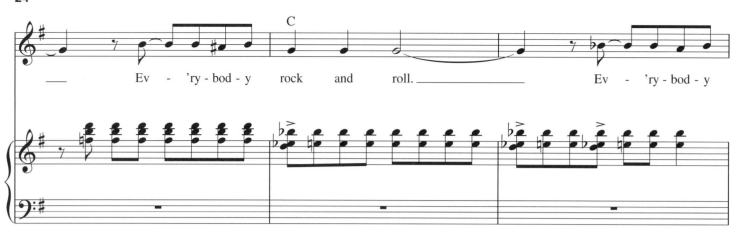

Ev - 'ry-bod - y rock and roll. _____ Ev - 'ry-bod - y

rock and roll. _____ Rock

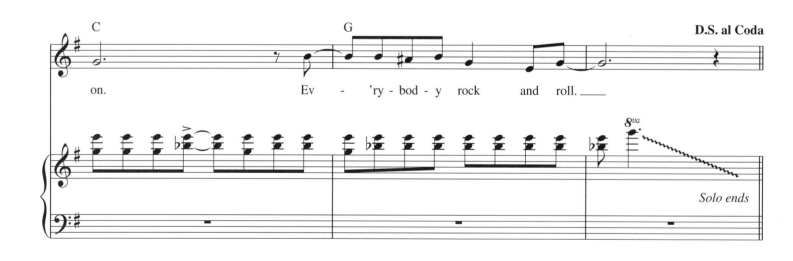

D.S. al Coda

on. Ev - 'ry-bod - y rock and roll. _____

Solo ends

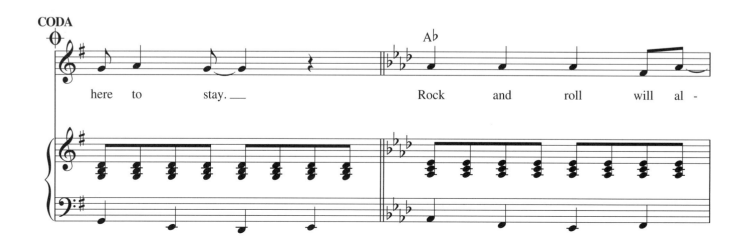

CODA

here to stay. ___ Rock and roll will al -

26

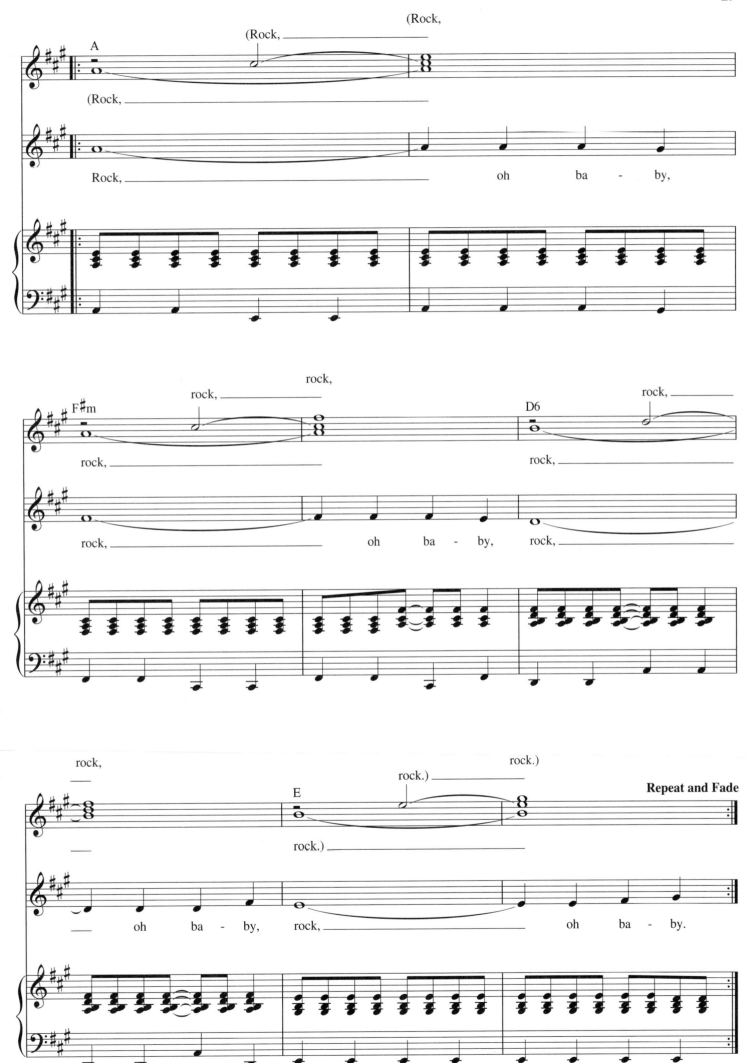

Shake, Rattle and Roll

Words and Music by Charles Calhoun

shake, rat - tle and roll. ___ Well, you nev - er do noth - in' to

save your dog - gone soul. _

Instrumental solo

Solo ends   I'm like a   one-eyed   cat ___   peep - in' in a   sea-food   store; ___
lieve   you're   do - in' me   wrong, ___ and ___ now I   know; ___

___   I'm like   a   one-eyed   cat ___   peep -
___   I   be - lieve   you're   do - in' me

Tutti Frutti

Words and Music by Little Richard Penniman and Dorothy La Bostrie

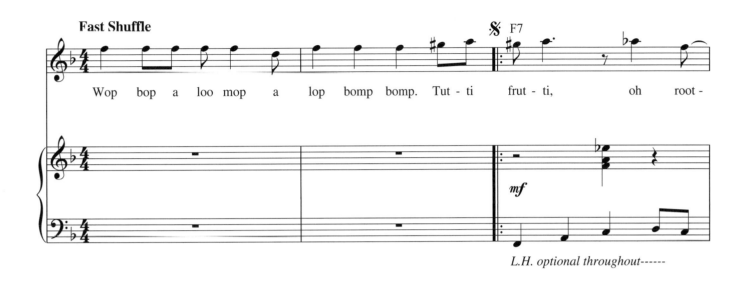

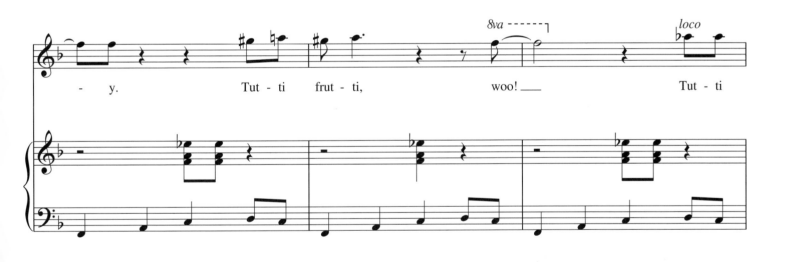

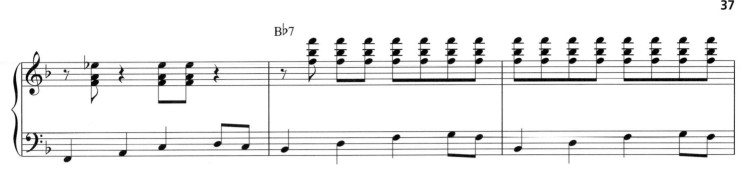

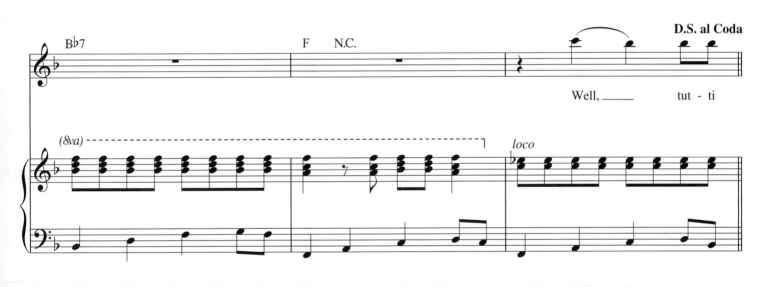

What'd I Say?

Words and Music by
Ray Charles

Hey, ma-ma, don't you treat me ___ wrong. Come and love your dad - dy
You see the girl ___ with the dia-mond ring? ___ She knows ___ how ___ to

all night long. ___ All right ___ now, hey ___
shake that thing. ___ All right ___ now, hey ___

hey, all ___ right.
hey, hey ___ hey.

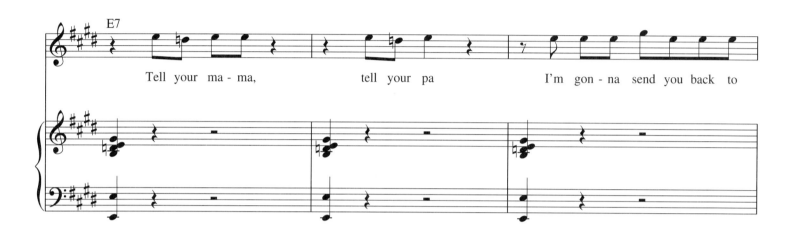

Tell your ma - ma, tell your pa I'm gon - na send you back to

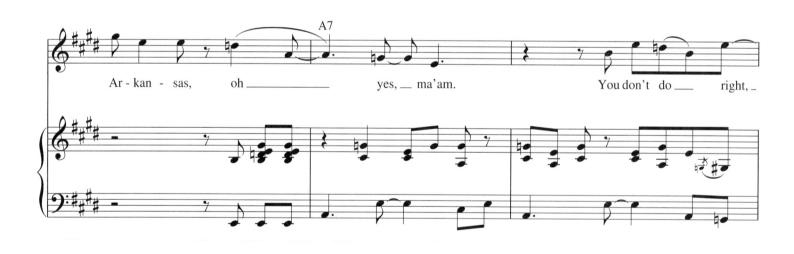

Ar - kan - sas, oh _____ yes, _ ma'am. You don't do _ right, _

_ don't do _ right. _

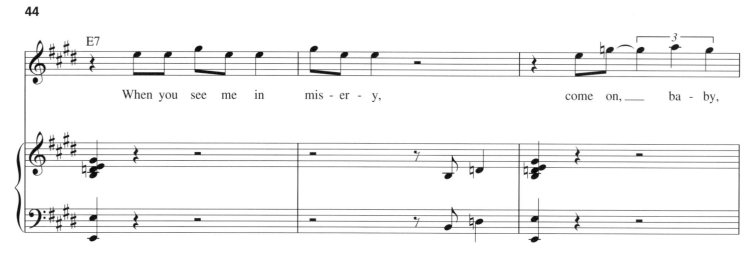

When you see me in mis-er-y, come on, ___ ba - by,

see a-bout me now, yeah. ___ Hey, ___

hey, all ___ right.

HAL•LEONARD® KEYBOARD PLAY-ALONG

The Keyboard Play-Along series will help you quickly and easily play your favorite songs as played by your favorite artists. Just follow the music in the book, listen to the CD to hear how the keyboard should sound, and then play along using the separate backing tracks. The melody and lyrics are also included in the book in case you want to sing, or simply to help you follow along. The audio CD is playable on any CD player. For PC and Mac users, the CD is enhanced so you can adjust the recording to any tempo without changing pitch! Each book/CD pack in this series features eight great songs.

1. POP/ROCK HITS
Against All Odds (Take a Look at Me Now) (Phil Collins) • Deacon Blues (Steely Dan) • (Everything I Do) I Do It for You (Bryan Adams) • Hard to Say I'm Sorry (Chicago) • Kiss on My List (Hall & Oates) • My Life (Billy Joel) • Walking in Memphis (Marc Cohn) • What a Fool Believes (The Doobie Brothers).
00699875 Keyboard Transcriptions $14.95

2. SOFT ROCK
Don't Know Much (Aaron Neville) • Glory of Love (Peter Cetera) • I Write the Songs (Barry Manilow) • It's Too Late (Carole King) • Just Once (James Ingram) • Making Love Out of Nothing at All (Air Supply) • We've Only Just Begun (Carpenters) • You Are the Sunshine of My Life (Stevie Wonder).
00699876 Keyboard Transcriptions $12.95

3. CLASSIC ROCK
Against the Wind (Bob Seger) • Come Sail Away (Styx) • Don't Do Me like That (Tom Petty and the Heartbreakers) • Jessica (Allman Brothers) • Say You Love Me (Fleetwood Mac) • Takin' Care of Business (Bachman-Turner Overdrive) • Werewolves of London (Warren Zevon) • You're My Best Friend (Queen).
00699877 Keyboard Transcriptions $14.95

4. CONTEMPORARY ROCK
Angel (Sarah McLachlan) • Beautiful (Christina Aguilera) • Because of You (Kelly Clarkson) • Don't Know Why (Norah Jones) • Fallin' (Alicia Keys) • Listen to Your Heart (D.H.T.) • A Thousand Miles (Vanessa Carlton) • Unfaithful (Rihanna).
00699878 Keyboard Transcriptions $12.95

5. ROCK HITS
Back at One (Brian McKnight) • Brick (Ben Folds) • Clocks (Coldplay) • Drops of Jupiter (Tell Me) (Train) • Home (Michael Buble) • 100 Years (Five for Fighting) • This Love (Maroon 5) • You're Beautiful (James Blunt)
00699879 Keyboard Transcriptions $14.95

6. ROCK BALLADS
Bridge over Troubled Water (Simon & Garfunkel) • Easy (Commodores) • Hey Jude (Beatles) • Imagine (John Lennon) • Maybe I'm Amazed (Paul McCartney) • A Whiter Shade of Pale (Procol Harum) • You Are So Beautiful (Joe Cocker) • Your Song (Elton John).
00699880 Keyboard Transcriptions $14.95

7. ROCK CLASSICS
Baba O'Riley (The Who) • Bloody Well Right (Supertramp) • Carry on Wayward Son (Kansas) • Changes (David Bowie) • Cold As Ice (Foreigner) • Evil Woman (Electric Light Orchestra) • Space Truckin' (Deep Purple) • That's All (Genesis).
00699881 Keyboard Transcriptions $14.95

8. BILLY JOEL – CLASSICS
Angry Young Man • Captain Jack • Honesty • Movin' Out (Anthony's Song) • My Life • Only the Good Die Young • Piano Man • Summer, Highland Falls.
00700302 Keyboard Transcriptions $14.99

9. ELTON JOHN BALLADS
Blue Eyes • Candle in the Wind • Daniel • Don't Let the Sun Go Down on Me • Goodbye Yellow Brick Road • Rocket Man (I Think It's Gonna Be a Long Long Time) • Someone Saved My Life Tonight • Sorry Seems to Be the Hardest Word.
00700752 Keyboard Transcriptions $14.99

11. THE DOORS
Break on Through to the Other Side • Hello, I Love You (Won't You Tell Me Your Name?) • L.A. Woman • Light My Fire • Love Me Two Times • People Are Strange • Riders on the Storm • Roadhouse Blues.
00699886 Keyboard Transcriptions $14.95

12. CHRISTMAS HITS
Baby, It's Cold Outside (Tom Jones & Cerys Matthews) • Blue Christmas (Elvis Presley) • Merry Christmas, Darling (Carpenters) • Mistletoe and Wine (Cliff Richard) • Santa Baby (Eartha Kitt) • A Spaceman Came Travelling (Chris de Burgh) • Step into Christmas (Elton John) • Wonderful Christmastime (Paul McCartney).
00700267 Keyboard Transcriptions $14.95

13. BILLY JOEL – HITS
Allentown • Just the Way You Are • New York State of Mind • Pressure • Root Beer Rag • Scenes from an Italian Restaurant • She's Always a Woman • Tell Her About It.
00700303 Keyboard Transcriptions $14.99

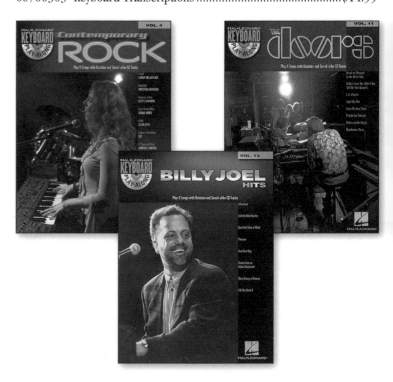

FOR MORE INFORMATION, SEE YOUR LOCAL MUSIC DEALER, OR WRITE TO:

HAL•LEONARD® CORPORATION
7777 W. BLUEMOUND RD. P.O. BOX 13819 MILWAUKEE, WI 53213

Visit Hal Leonard Online at
www.halleonard.com

Prices, contents, and availability subject to change without notice.

0809